Amy Carmichael

From the fight

Amy Carmichael

From the fight

ISBN/EAN: 9783337135355

Printed in Europe, USA, Canada, Australia, Japan

Cover: Foto ©ninafisch / pixelio.de

More available books at **www.hansebooks.com**

From the Fight

By
AMY
WILSON-CARMICHAEL

(*C.E.Z. "KESWICK" MISSIONARY, INDIA*),

Author of "Sunrise Land," *etc.*

With Original Drawings by F. A. Baker.

———◆———

London:
CHURCH OF ENGLAND ZENANA MISSIONARY SOCIETY,
27, Chancery Lane, W.C.

MARSHALL BROTHERS,
Keswick House, Paternoster Row, E.C.

TRANSLATION.

"His sacred form is Love,
His holy eye is the deep home of Grace,
His blessed word, distilling as the dew,
Is life's Elixir, truest, purest joy.
He looks upon the world of sinful men,
And stretches out His hand to beckon them.
His hand, so glad to give, so strong to guard,
And then, it is as if He said, 'Fear not.'

"Why wander weary still?
Why wilfully go sad?   Oh, people come!
Come all ye people, to the succouring feet
Of Him Who is alone your own true Lord.
Is your heart iron?   Has it not melted yet?
Oh, turn ye but a little, look to Him
Th' renouncing God, Who gave His life for you.
And, won by looking, come to Him Who calls
And longs that you should live!"

    KRISHNA PILLÁI,
     Convert, Scholar, and Poet,
      Tinnevelley, S. India,
       Went in to see the King
        January, 1900.

The Beginning

THIS little book is a piece of patchwork. It is made of bits from the "Life of Faith," bits from "India's Women," bits from Home Letters, and bits written for itself. Pen patchwork of a truth. This explains its broken and fragmentary character. It is only Bits of Things. But it has been asked for, so it goes as it is.

Out in the Fight, where fighting comes first and writing second, there is no time to write as one ought for that serious thing called Print; but will you ask the Great Captain to use it to make the fight real to some of His soldiers at

FROM THE FIGHT.

home? We need more troops out here. Not one garrison, not one regiment, is anything like full-manned.

These letters do not touch upon the work among the Christians, to which much of our strength is given; neither do they touch upon life in New India—the India of the Schools. We live in the heart of Old India—it is a dark Old India, very sinful, very needy, needing God.

The dear friend in whose home on the hills these scraps have been strung together, says that she never reads the headings of chapters, and skips all poetry contained therein. In case anyone who reads this inclines to do so, may I say, for once, please do not! because the chapter headings have something to do with what is inside the chapters—at least they may help to throw light upon the nature of the people of whom the chapters tell. They are like *looks in*. And the fragments of verse in the last two chapters are meant to be just the same. Look *in* with eyes anointed with the sympathy of Jesus. Look *out* again—look upon the fields—

FROM THE FIGHT.

and then, oh! we plead with you, look *up*—
"Lord, what wilt Thou have me to do?"

Yours in the Fight,
Looking for the coming
of the Conqueror,

Amy Wilson-Carmichael.

TIRUNELVÉLI JILLAH,
S. INDIA,
April, 1900.

CONTENTS.

CHAPTER.		PAGE.
I.	Indoors	6
II.	Out of Doors	17
III.	Caste and Custom...	28
IV.	Sorrow and Suffering	39
V.	Phases of Thought	51

CHAPTER I.

INDOORS.

"Show good to the Good—the Responsive,
And in rock that abideth you write it:
Show good to the Bad—Unresponsive,
In wavering water indite it.
    Impressions abide, or impressions fade,
    As the heart is, so the impression made."
            AVVAYÂR,
                Tamil Poetess,
                    A thousand years ago.

"FROM the Fight," for it *is* a fight. A fight without one iota of the romantic. A downright real fight. And we are only soldiers "standing in the ranks, having no right to think, no right to question, but the solitary right to do what the Captain says, come what may."

"A village bright enough to the outward eye." *See page 7.*

FROM THE FIGHT.

But fight though it is, the battle is the Lord's, and victory will come with the Morning.

It is not Morning yet.

See this. A village, bright enough to the outward eye, for here instead of wild jungle waste, we have a bit of God's beauty let down on the sand—but a village enchained, enslaved, wrapped round in thick darkness.

There are temple fortresses there, and shrines, and idols, and idol cars. And the men and women and children, too, are stamped with the stamp of the devil-god, a mark painted clear on the brow. You pass through the streets, where no one will stop to think across to the life to come. You visit a house (a caste-house, where confession of Christ would mean the literal loss of all things), and find the women gathered within, waiting for you. And now what have you to do? Tell the glad tidings gladly to hearts that are glad to hear? That is ideal, truly, but the real is not like that. Not one is keen to hear. Not one is longing or hungry. They like you to come, it is true. You come as a break in the day. And they will listen a little —but care? Ah no—not yet.

But you gather round the lamp, a pretty thing hung with flowers, and you try to find if they know what you talked about to them last time. Then you tell them a little more, and

FROM THE FIGHT.

plead with them as you can—and then interruptions come. There is no shut door to them here! For first the husband arrives and causes a general stir, and then the mother-in-law has something to say, and great is the fidget and fuss; and then a baby cries, and has to be petted and shaken; and so it goes on, and you feel almost baffled; for how can the Still Voice speak through such noisy restlessness? *Our* voices grow weary enough, and our hearts grow wearier still, for it seems like fighting shadows, till the remembrance suddenly comes—Not shadow, but substance, the great grim substance of Satanic opposition. And then we take courage again—for the battle is the Lord's.

The husband sees us home. He is like polished marble. Nothing seems to *go in*. He knows the truth, but meets it with a smile. Only the power of the Spirit can make that mountain flow. Our homeward way brings us through a crowd of idolaters. They are marrying their god and goddess. Torches blaze, and excited beings dance to the thud of the tom-tom. Incense thickens the air. The scent and the smoke, and the glare and the blare follow us far down the street. And we marvel at the patience of God.

* * *

FROM THE FIGHT.

A week later.

We have been there this evening again. May God help us to tell you of it, if by telling you we may help you to pray, as we want you to pray, as we *need* you to pray for us!

For to-night it was utterly sad. They had been worshipping—what do you think? That *lamp* we chanced to mention before as being so pretty with flowers. We did not know what the flowers meant then—God's desecrated flowers! Yes, they had prayed to the lamp, or to the light in it, rather; they had used the very words we had taught them to say to our God if they wanted His help, a little prayer asking for light to enlighten their darkness—strangest of strange prayers surely, to pray to the light their own hands had kindled! They had painted their foreheads then with the sacred ashes, and they were just fresh from it all when we came to talk to them.

The mother, who led the prayer, as she knew it best, sat near. She had her child in her arms, a dear little loving child. We asked her what she would feel if her little one ran away, and clung to some stranger woman, and would not come back to her. For answer, she clasped her close, and closer, and closer still. We tried to tell her then of the Fatherheart of God.

Oh, these Jericho walls of strong superstition

FROM THE FIGHT.

and sin! Sometimes it seems as though the soul is a city walled up to heaven, and a city roofed over, too, for the gentle grace of the Lord seems to fall upon cold grey slate.

Do you ever pray, as you pray for these, *that the Spirit would create in them what is not there now—true soul-thirst after God?*

Do you pray that they may so know their need that the cry as of pain, the cry of life, may rise from hearts which are silent towards Him, still, silent—silent as death?

One afternoon we were visiting in the same caste village, the Village of the Lake. "Caste" —that word means much. "The one hundred and fifty millions of caste Hindus still present to Christianity an unbroken front, or very little broken, apparently." In this caste village there is not one inquirer among the men, and only two among the women. To visit in that village is to fight the devil straight.

We had been at it for some hours, going from house to house, and from courtyard to courtyard, speaking to any who would listen, and looking, looking ever for one who *cared* to hear. We did not find one. "We do not want your God, we do not want your Way"—all said it in one form or another, and this was all.

We had come to the last house, a goldsmith's, wherein abode an old blind woman, a widow and a wife. Two of the three had never heard before, and the very words we had to use were unfamiliar. They had no wish to understand, which made it harder to explain. At last they went away, tired of even the novelty of "the foolishness of preaching."

Where are the heathen who are "longing for the Gospel"? Oh, to see one, *even one*, in whose heart is a hunger and a thirst after God!

We were left alone with the wife. Something almost wistful in her dull and dreary face made us ask her if she were happy. Happy! with no children and a husband like hers? Then we told her more of Him Who is the Crown of our Joy.

She seemed to turn towards Him just a little then; pushing out a hand, it seemed, in some poor timid fashion, to feel after Him in the dark. We could not be sure, but we trusted so, and left her with Him Who is not far from every one of us.

But oh! the tempest which will burst upon her should this tiny flicker burn into a flame! She must go through it all alone.

Two evenings later we went again. Yes, she had meant what she said that day; she told us she wanted to come to our Saviour—but she could not tell her husband. She dare not.

We stood with her in the courtyard, half in

FROM THE FIGHT.

moonlight, half in shadow, the long fringed fronds of a cocoanut palm, all silver tipped, beyond the wall, and one glorious star shone far above. And she knelt with us as we prayed for courage for her, and faith. Suddenly she shivered, "My husband!" she said, "he is coming." We had to go and leave her in her loneliness.

*   *

It is hard for the widows and wives; it is harder still for the girls. Here is one whom we often see, a girl for whom many have worked and prayed. She has faced the cost, and is ready now to confess her Lord in baptism. She has told her mother about it; and her brothers, to whom she owes all submission, know it too, though she has not told them herself, and are hurrying on a marriage by way of counter force. So it seems a case of "Now or never" for her. They are trying to frighten her, and shake her strange resolve, and we went to strengthen her in the Lord and the power of His might.

Her people knew we were coming, and were very excited and noisy; but we walked straight through the crowd which had gathered in the courtyard—not a hand raised to stop us—to the inner room where, hidden behind half a dozen relations, the girl was waiting for us.

FROM THE FIGHT.

We had a good time with her, in spite of the noise outside. There was nothing at all between save a scrap of palm leaf trellis, so the hammering which the two brothers indulged in, with more than Indian energy, and the hubbub of voices—*that*, at least, was thoroughly Indian—seemed to break like rough waves round us; but there was peace in the midst of it all, and the dark little room was light.

Then we talked to the mother awhile, and asked her to let her child follow the Master Who called her. But, no! "Would she destroy our caste and disgrace us all? Ungrateful that she is! Be baptised? No! Never! Never!"

"Shall we speak to your brothers?" we asked. She hesitated a moment. It was bringing things to a crisis. But our God is a God of Truth, and all His work is above-board; so, after a minute's fear—for she knew far better than I what this open avowal might mean—she said very bravely, "*Yes.*"

These brothers—her father is dead—are practically all-powerful as regards her life and future. They are bitterly hostile, most bigoted Hindus. Earnestly asking for words, we went outside to the men.

They were very polite at first, and so were all the relations; but soon they dropped disguise, and said what they meant, which was this:

FROM THE FIGHT.

"Baptised! [That is always the crux, because it involves loss of caste]. She shall burn to ashes first. She may go out dead if she likes. She shall go out living—*never!*"

And the girl inside heard it all.

We went back again to her. The glow of the little red fire lit up her eyes, and we saw they shone steadfast and strong.

Then we had to go away! If only we might have stayed and shared what might follow with her! But no; she must bear it alone.

Or if we could have taken her home—carried her off in the face of the whole street up in arms. But that would be kidnapping, a "first-class" misdemeanour. For the difficulty is this: We have not her horoscope, which would prove her to be of age to come to us. Her people have hidden it, and will not let her see it. We have no proof which would stand in the law courts, and though we believe her to be old enough to choose her own guardians (which is the view the law takes of such matters), a hundred false witnesses would be ready to be bribed to swear she was not.

And so we can do nothing for her. Unless some interposition occur, she is doomed to marry a heathen, with all the involvings therein. And we are helpless to hinder. If one did not know beyond a doubt "standeth God amid the

FROM THE FIGHT.

shadows, keeping watch above His own," one's heart would utterly fail.

* * *

If this chapter closed here, the impression left would be either too dark or too bright. So, for the sake of truthfulness, I add a few words now.

The mother, who led the prayer to the lamp, using the words we had taught her to say to the Light of the World—Has she turned, and come to Him yet? No; she grows harder and harder. And now the house is closed.

The wife, who did seem to come—Has she gone on? For a little while she did, but her husband frightened her back. One night she felt him stirring beside her; she opened her eyes, and saw a dagger gleaming. "Turn Christian—and expect *this!*" he whispered in her ear. She compromised then, and lost ground at once. "He that is stedfast . . . shall attain unto life." She has not been a stedfast soul.

And the girl? If we did not love her as we do, we might tell her story now. But we dare not expose her to the danger of print just yet. Satan seems to make a dead set upon anyone—more especially a convert—who is too soon "put in print." But to the glory of our God we may say that He did deliver her. And He has kept

FROM THE FIGHT.

her safe and true through all that has happened since. Her coming out has shut the caste houses for many a mile all round us, but He has worked behind the locked doors; and "with Him is strength and effectual working."

So not too dark must our story be, for we are on the winning side; and yet it must not be too bright, for few fight through to victory.

CHAPTER II.

OUT OF DOORS.

"Love, knowledge, power, and chosen words, three things
Should he possess who speaks the word of kings.
An envoy meet is he, well learned, of fearless eye,
Who speaks right home, prepared for each emergency."

TIRUVULLUVAR,
Tamil Poet,
A thousand years ago.
From Dr. Pope's Translation.

HAVE you time to turn over one more leaf in the book of heathendom? It is a big book, and black. Every page a black page, only here and there crossed with a line of white. And the little white makes the great black seem all the blacker. Oh! for the day when upon our

FROM THE FIGHT.

poor world's night the light shall break as the morning!—"A morning without clouds."

It is a Hindu Festival Day. See the people streaming by thousands to the temple of the demon goddess by the river. They are all leading goats; 2,900 were slaughtered last year. Perhaps about as many are doomed to die to-morrow. They will dash water upon the creature's head. If it shivers it is slain, if it does not it escapes. But the main thought in the carnage soon to be is, or was in its origin, the expiation of sin. "Neither by the blood of goats and calves"—they do not know that yet.

We are standing midway in the dried-up river bed. It is very wide. Innumerable groups, each composed of hundreds, are scattered about from side to side, and as far away down as the eye can reach.

See them! all unheeding, and unthinking, bent upon enjoyment only, outwardly a happy people, meeting for a holiday. Here and there is one not quite so jubilant—a woman, with an offering which means that she is childless, and appealing to the goddess; a devotee, with more thoughtful or more wicked expression; a lad from some village mission school, who sees through the tinsel, and knows there is no gold behind.

Built up on the bank rises the demon

FROM THE FIGHT.

temple. Its striped red and white walls stand square and strong as if nothing could ever shake them. Idolatry is something tangible here; terribly so.

And there are we, a tiny band of a dozen to thousands backed by the principalities and powers and the rulers of the darkness of this world, and spiritual wickedness in high places. But—with us is the God of battles. We had prayed beforehand that they should be moved to listen, and even buy our Gospels — this last seeming most improbable. But they listen, and they buy, and we thank Him and take courage. See them—men, chiefly, but here and there a woman and child—see them sitting on the sand, circled, again, by the less interested, standing. We, with our bullock carts ranged as background, facing them, holding forth to them the Word of Life. We did not see any one taking it then—but we "*believe* to see."

After two such meetings and divers raids in among the crowd, it was time to go. And we left them, sadly feeling we had barely touched the fringe, and yet praising Him for the chance of letting the standard fly right in the face of the foe. Next year, if the Lord tarry, we hope to go earlier and camp out, and do the thing more thoroughly. This sort of surface work is like playing with souls.

FROM THE FIGHT.

Next day we met them as they returned, their carts horrible with the extended bodies of the victims, their faces the more wicked or more weary for the past night's revelry. And yet—" ye will not come to Me that ye might have life!"

Oh! it is a real fight—this Indian fight for souls! We must have a daily re-inspiration, or we shall lose courage and fail. But we need not fail, we shall not; for however tremendous the odds against us, God Himself is with us for our Captain—the King of Glory—the Lord mighty in battle!

Of course, wherever we possibly can, we try to get into the houses, and talk to the women alone. This is by far the best way to get at them; here, as elsewhere, it is soul to soul dealing which tells.

But in Pioneer work this is sometimes quite out of the question. We go to towns and villages where no white women have ever been seen, and where no caste woman will open her door; and then we are forced to stand in the streets, and go in for an "Open Air."

We always get groups of women, and any number of children, but never any young girls. They are shut up inside. There is often much opposition, and the seed seems thrown away; but we think of Him Who preached by the wayside, and "at the head of the noisy streets . . .

FROM THE FIGHT.

at the entering in of the gates," and we rest on the strong "*shall doubtless*" of the promise of our God.

Pictures of this sort of work may not be prettily painted. M. Coillard, in his book, "On the Threshold of Central Africa," writes that "it needs to be known that the soldier of Christ does not gather the laurels of his crown of life in a delightful garden, where he can tread the primrose paths in velvet slippers." Every missionary knows how true that is.

As I write in the restful cool and quiet of the hills, scene after scene rises before me. We are down in the burning plains—we are holding an "Open-Air." See the scoffing faces; hear the revilings rained upon us as we close. What has stirred up such a sea of scathing scorn? *The proclamation of the coming of the King.* They cannot stand that. Satan hates the very echo of that song. He drowns it now in the olden cry, "Away with Him! Away with Him! Crucify Him! Crucify Him!"

See us again. This time no opposition worth the name. Only dull apathy, utterly unmoved indifference. Oh, for a face with a soul in it! Oh, for one gleam of response! But dully, dully they turn away, and sadly, sadly we watch them. Can these bones live? Oh, Lord, Thou knowest!

FROM THE FIGHT.

Again—and we are in the Village of the Prince, with the bright morning light making everything beautiful, and filling one's soul with a sort of light-gladness as one looks and feels, and enjoys it all.

We have had a woman's meeting at one end of the village, while the men held one at the other end, and now the crowd is beginning to melt, when a woman springs across the path, and confronts us angrily. Something tells us she must be a devil-dancer; she is so fierce and wild. Her hair is matted and twisted in cords, and hanging about her face. Her forehead is marked with the vile idol marks in spots and smears and stripes. Round her neck is a necklet soaked in some dye, and dabs of saffron all over her face furthermore help to disguise and deform her. When this apparition appears the crowd gathers quickly again, expecting a scene, and the woman, gesturing fearfully, makes a rush for us, and begins:—" Oh, your God is no god! If I came to Him my own devil-god would kill me! He is god! He is god! But yours you say died—died as a criminal, too! Oh, go! quickly go, and tell your lies in the villages further away,—who asks you to tell them here?"

The crowd applauds. They are all caste people; they would think it far too defiling to let us come into their houses — for we are breaking new ground just now, and have not yet won our way—but they look at this dreadful creature with eyes of approval, and say, "She has answered you well, now go! For who has seen Heaven and who has seen hell? *She* knows, and you don't; now go!"

We told her the true God loved her, but she laughed a horrid laugh; we tried and tried again to get one ray of sunshine in, but the shutters were shut too close.

Oh, if we could only *show* them His love! Surely if they could see it they could not resist Him so! Poor souls, they do not know; and what can they know with one hearing? But we have to leave them and go on and on, for in hundreds and hundreds of villages still the women have never heard.

And yet sometimes, when they often hear, they *will* not come to Him. They push away those gentle hands, which are "all day long stretched forth" to them. And that is the saddest thing we have in Heathendom. But—I quote from Dr. Moule, whose words in his book on the Epistle to the Romans often come home to us here—"the servant brings his sorrows for consolation—may we write the words in reverence? —the sorrows of his Master. He mourns over an Athens, an Ephesus, and, above all, over a

FROM THE FIGHT.

Jerusalem, that will not come to the Son of God, that they might have life. And his grief is not only inevitable, it is profoundly right, wise, holy. But he need not bear it unrelieved. He grasps the Scripture which tells him that his Lord has called those who would not come, and opened the eternal arms for an embrace—to be met only with a contradiction. He weeps, but it is as on the breast of Jesus as He wept over the city; and in the double certainty that the Lord has felt such grief, and that HE IS THE LORD, he yields, he rests, he is still. The King of the ages and the Man of sorrows are One. To know Him is to be at peace even under the griefs of the mystery of sin."

* * *

The interruptions in Open Air work are legion. You have just got your audience in hand when a bullock cart rumbles round, and the group breaks up to let it pass, and it may not incline to form again. Or, worse still, if it is evening, a herd of cows, perhaps fifty strong, with their calves, and as many buffaloes, each bent on making its way straight to its own habitation regardless of obstruction, tramples through the throng. Perhaps you have been deep in your subject, and did not notice anything till a cloud of dust, and a medley of horns and hoofs, and a scattering of your audience, and your ideas too,

A Hook-Swinging Festival.

FROM THE FIGHT.

apprises you of the advent of these intelligent creatures. "The ox knoweth his owner, and the ass his master's crib," is a verse familiar by dire experience to all South Indian preachers. One evening I was sitting on the doorstep of a house, with a dozen women round me, when suddenly a beast appeared, and without a moment's hesitation it walked straight over me, and in.

Then, often a caste row acts as devil's interrupter. A high-caste woman thinks some low-caste woman has touched her, or that she will if she does not remonstrate. So she remonstrates. Sometimes an amiable friend will scatter some cayenne pepper in your too near vicinity, or she will find it expedient to cook it, and the smoke makes you cough and choke, and this has a disturbing effect. There are always small infants who cry, and bigger infants who laugh, and there are noises, of course, of every conceivable kind without much intermission. For we are on the enemy's ground, and the harder we mean to fight him the harder he will fight us.

But then we have such a wonderful God; He can use interruptions even to hold the souls He will win. A few months ago we were working in a village of eight thousand Hindus. We were in the middle of an Open Air, near the well where the caste people came to draw water,

FROM THE FIGHT.

when a madman began to make a disturbance, and we feared the meeting was spoilt. But only a few weeks ago we heard that one who had come to draw water was on the point of moving away when this little break occurred, and she lingered to see what would happen. While she waited words caught her ear. They were new and strange to her. But "He opened my mind to understand," as she put it herself when she told it, and to-day she is His, we trust, and His to be used to win others.

But this is not a usual thing. Not often does the first hearing mean more than the dimmest conception of the meaning of the message— only, sometimes, perhaps to remind us that His name is really WONDERFUL, He does do something "wondrously," and we and our band look on.

But every battle of the warrior is with confused noise, and garments rolled in blood. It is not lightly souls are won. We are not speaking of so-called mass movements towards Christianity among the lower orders—a thing we wholly distrust, but of *individual conversions to Christ* among men and women, high or low in social status, and especially are we thinking of conversions among those who, by their very position as members of caste are entrenched within the central citadel of Hinduism. No

FROM THE FIGHT.

words can give you the least conception of what caste is in this part of India. It is the very stronghold of the devil, rooted as a living thing upon the rock of an ancient creed, moated by the mighty moat of custom, buttressed by the landmarks of superstition, hoary with the ages. Here it stands, strong as ever, and only in the far vision of faith have we seen its proud walls fall.

Sometimes, as we stand in the shadow of the portal of some great old temple, we all repeat together our battle verse.

"The weapons of our warfare are not carnal, but mighty through God to the pulling down of strongholds," ("to their utter demolition," in Tamil,) "casting down imaginations and every high thing that exalteth itself against the knowledge of God."

Oh the glorious force of such a verse! It nerves one and inspires one to believe to see the hand of the Lord stretching forth to mightily deliver.

CHAPTER III.

CASTE AND CUSTOM.

"There is no people upon the face of the earth who are afflicted with so many self-imposed, and therefore remediable, evils as the Hindus."

Sir Madhává Rau,
An educated Brahman.

"OSHA"; "Murrévu"—what do these words mean?

A month ago a comrade-friend on the hills told us about a young wife whom she was visiting. "Her limbs are being slowly twisted up with rheumatism. They want to try a quack medicine, but are too poor to afford it; or rather her husband does not care enough to be willing to spend anything upon her. And after all it would not do any

FROM THE FIGHT.

good. It is sunshine she wants, and that is just what she cannot get. *She is Gosha.*"

One day she took me to see her. She lives in a room facing north, and walled in on the south, so that no sunshine ever enters it. The floor was damp that day; she was crouching on it, but rose as we went in. A woman with a sweet wan face which must have been beautiful once, but the shadow of Gosha had crossed it, and stamped the beauty out. Now it is full of pain, though so patient. One's very heart ached for her. She showed us her poor hands, twisting, thickening at the joints. She spoke of the medicine, and my friend told her again it was *sunshine* she needed. She shook her head: "*I am Gosha.*"

There outside was the sunshine, shining straight down as it does out here, where the sun rides overhead. Within two steps from her door it was filling the street with its warmth and light. Only two steps away, yet utterly out of her reach. For she must live shut up inside. This is what *Gosha* means.

And there she is, fading away like a flower in the dark. Who cares if she pine and die? Her husband can get another wife—wives are cheap in India. Nobody cares what happens to her, if only the Gosha laws are fulfilled—for that to them is everything. Oh, this terrible Gosha!

FROM THE FIGHT.

One realised the power of Mahommedanism afresh, even if only viewed from an external point of view, as we stepped out into God's free sunshine, so near her, yet so far away, and left her behind—in prison.

Of the spiritual antitype I need not speak. It is so evident. But just for a moment think of her. When you read these lines she will most likely be just as she was that day—only perhaps suffering more, as the weary pain gains ground inch by inch. Think of the system which shuts her down, fastens her on the rack, holds her there, kills her, should she wish to be free. "*We take it all too easily, far too easily. We see them perishing, and we know they are perishing; but yet we go about our ordinary avocations as though there were no such thing as perishing people, and as though we could not do infinitely more than we are doing to try to save them!*"

* * *

Murrévu—another language, and meaning Gosha, so to speak, for a prescribed time, differing according to caste. What Gosha is in Mahommedan work, Murrévu is in work among Hindu caste-women and girls. And caste is a thing with an iron hand: it grips, and it grips to the death.

We were missioning in a large Hindu town a few weeks ago, when we came across a girl-widow of eighteen, a very fair girl, with luminous, starlike eyes, and a cloud of wavy hair. We heard her story. Oh, the pathos of it!

A little while since she was married; within twenty days she was widowed. They took her beautiful silks away, and her precious jewels and trinkets, and robed her in the widow's white —the hated, dreaded white! Then she sat and wept, and wailed. "Oh, my husband! my Lord! the light of my life, my heart's desire! you have left me swinging in empty space. I look all round; I see you not! I wander hither and thither in vain. Oh! sinner that I am! There is no comforter!"

And so the days passed, for she must never cease to mourn, and fast, and weep, if haply the sin, her mysterious other-birth sin, about which she often wonders, may be forgiven her.

It was so we found her. She was sitting in the little house doing nothing, just mourning for her dead.

We showed her the Wordless Book. Her eyes lit over the gold-leaf page, and she said: "Is there a way to that Golden City (one of their names for Heaven). Is there a way by which I can go? Oh, tell me!"

We seldom hear this sort of question; I had never heard it before, and it flashed across one's mind: Would she come with us and learn?

There were such possibilities open, if only she would! We asked her. Her mother might come, too, we said. (They live alone together—two widows.) They could learn then every day, and very soon they would know the way to the Golden City.

The girl was leaning forward, her dark eyes shining with excitement. She turned to her mother. "*Mother!*" she said, half breathlessly. For a moment no one spoke. Could this daring thing come true? Oh, *would* they come?

Then, "*She is in Murrévu.*" Not another word. It was enough. We asked "For how long?" "*For twelve whole years.* She may not go out even to draw water. She is in strict Murrévu. It is our custom."

Again we went to see her, and again she listened heart and soul, as it seemed, to the good tidings of great joy, meant for her, even for her, a widow; but a question arose about caste. Slowly the awful involvings dawned upon them. The mother broke out in lament. "Would you steal my daughter from me? Would you leave me to die without her? Shall my eye grow weary with longing? Must they fail with watching for her? Faint, I shall cry for water; but thirsty I shall lie! And *this* is your good religion! Alas! that you call it good!"

Still she listened, and still we prayed, and we

marvelled that the house was kept open, for one such visit usually shuts the door, and once shut it rarely opens again.

One evening the girl asked: "Could you not come every day?" We had to tell her we could not. There are so many other towns, and many, many villages, and we have no one to send to them. She said: "Come *every day* when you come to our town;" and we promised indeed we would. The mother smiled grimly, and said: "Don't think you are going to win her! She is in Murrévu, so how could she be a Christian?"

Then, as if to prove the absurdity of it she pointed to the verandah running round the house; "See! she may not even put her foot upon *that*; so how could she be a Christian?"

We pleaded with her; but no. "My heart is stone when you talk of your God; talk as far as you may, not an atom moves within me."

Next time we went the girl was gone. The old mother watched our disappointed faces with malicious delight, explaining how her daughter had gone to her mother-in-law's to a great feast, and would not be back for a few days. Where is the mother-in-law's village? "Oh, a long way off to the west." "Its name?" She smiled as she answered. The village she mentioned does not exist. We saw further questions

FROM THE FIGHT.

were useless. The answers were all to put us off the track. The girl was gone. That was all we knew for certain.

But after a while she became less wary, and by mistake the truth came out. It was just what we had expected. The mother-in-law heard of our visits and came down upon the mother for letting us come. "Oh! we had such a family fight! She tore me with her words. She told me about you. How you went to two caste houses such as this, and dusted magic powder on two girls' faces, and they broke caste, and fell into the pit of Christianity, and you bewitched them still further, and took off their jewels and sold them; and now you are going to marry them to low caste men"—a flight of imagination, this. "Oh, it is very bad! How could you do such things? So she took my daughter away by night, shut up in a covered cart, and nobody here knew. So her Murrévu is not broken. And she will always live with her mother-in-law, and you will never see her again!"

"But how sad for you! You will not see her either!" "Oh! yes, I shall. I see her every day. I saw her this morning." Then suddenly realising she was telling the truth she relapsed into lies, and we heard no more. But we concluded she is somewhere quite near, only hidden

FROM THE FIGHT.

as any girl here may be hidden, even if she is within one wall's distance from us.

As I write we are daily, hourly watching for the Lord to work for us concerning another girl, for truly we are shut up to waiting for Him. I have never once been allowed to see her because of the myth about the magic powder. Some of our workers have seen her for a minute or so at a time, and they say she is being kept wonderfully brave and true. Beyond this we know nothing, except that she is fighting against tremendous odds, with nothing to help her except a little Gospel of St. Matthew which we managed to send her, and which she keeps hidden in her dress, and reads when she has the chance. She is in strict Murrévu, too, and still more in very strict guard. She is never alone day or night for one moment, lest she should escape to us.

She believes herself to be of age, but cannot prove it, and we have reason to know that we cannot, and all the other castes have for once combined, and tell her that if she dares to disgrace herself, her family, and her village, by becoming a Christian, they will all unite and back up her parents in a lawsuit—and of course as false witnesses are cheap here (fourpence a head) any number will be found ready to swear away as many years as are required to prove her a

FROM THE FIGHT.

minor. I hardly like to write more of her yet. The issue is too uncertain. Twice she has been hurried away to a distant village. Once, at least, she has been seen crying under the lash. There is a cruel wrist-twisting torture in vogue here; she may have that to go through. But worst of all is the danger from the powers of evil all round her. Will she hold out? Will she give in? Oh! who will pray for a victory here, just where the fight is hottest?

And friends, as I write it, the thought comes —who among you who will read it can *really* pray? Surely only those who at all costs have given (if they could not come) to heathendom. Bishop Hill put it solemnly when he said: "*Look at the millions without Christ, and you will find an Altar. And may God help you to be a sacrifice!*"

Lastly, and will you not forgive this way of answering the thought which always seems to rise where God's altar comes into view: "Yes, *you* may sacrifice if you choose; but let those you love best sacrifice? Never! *Never at least, where it costs.*"

Three days ago in the late evening I stood by the side of one who was dying. The courtyard was full of people. They were all very still. The room was even more crowded. But no one spoke. They all watched. In the midst

FROM THE FIGHT.

lay the dying woman. She lay in mortal pain. Every breath was a stab, her hand was burning in fever. She could not speak, she just looked. Never shall I forget that look. Helpless, hopeless, utter fear! That long look haunts me still.

I had to leave her, and come home. An old man walked in front with a lantern. It was dark all round, and there was a great silence.

Then it seemed as if all nations, and kindreds, and peoples, and tongues of India were passing on towards a mighty gate. And they knew not what lay on the other side. But I knew that it was the Gate of Death.

There were very few to tell them so. Still, here and there were a few, and they turned some back from the Gate of Death.

Then the darkness lightened into day, and I saw, as it were, in a glory cloud, the passing on toward another Gate of *some who had given those few* to turn whom they could from the Gate of Death. And one (in the words of the old tale I tell it) "passed over, and all the trumpets sounded for him on the other side," and one to whom the way had been rough said as she neared the Gate: "However the weather is on my journey, I shall have time enough when I come there to sit down and rest me;" and so was comforted. And for all it was pure joy, for they knew what lay on the other side.

FROM THE FIGHT.

"And they had the city itself in view, and thought they heard all the bells therein to ring to welcome them thereto. Oh! by what tongue or pen can their glorious joy be expressed? Then they came up to the Gate."

And among the Shining Ones who met them were some whose faces beamed as they saw them, and they welcomed them with a special welcome, the words whereof I could not hear. But I saw that those who had entered in understood, and rejoiced with a wonderful joy, for they knew they had helped to fill Heaven.

And down on this lower earth a song seemed ringing sweet and clear :—

> "Oh! if one soul from India
> Meet *them* on God's right hand,
> *Their* Heaven would be ten Heavens
> In Emmanuel's Land!"

CHAPTER IV.

SORROW AND SUFFERING.

They march, and strike the note of pain,
A moment pause, then strike again;
A third time sounds the drummer's roll,
Mourning the passage of a soul.
A covered corpse—a torch of fire—
They bear it to the funeral pyre.
Ye mortals, look! the vision dread,
The dead go bearing forth their dead.

> THÂYUMANAVAR,
> *Tamil Poet,*
> *A thousand years ago.*

HE Indian woman is loving. She can love and she can hate, and so she can suffer too. She suffers in silence often—dumb, like the animals. She will not unveil her heart to the gaze of curious eyes. But when she knows you, and trusts you, she will let you look in through clear windows, and see her as she is.

FROM THE FIGHT.

There are some who mistake our people. They differ from us in expression of feeling, and so it is fancied they do not feel. "They are not a sensitive race," said one who had not the means of knowing *how* sensitive they are. There are points in their character which remind one of the poise of the aspen leaves. You know the delicate fashion the leaf is hung on its stalk. You know how a breath of wind, which hardly stirs the sturdier trees, is enough to set its leaves trembling, and you know how long it is before they are still again. And just so, what seems a mere nothing to us, will set a whole clan in motion, and every separate member thereof, like every separate leaf on the tree, vibrates with the common vibration.

A scholar and a lover of these people, Dr. Pope, of Oxford, writes how in many ways we fail to understand them. "Hindus are spoken of as apathetic. I should term them fervid." This "fervidness" enters into everything, perhaps most evidently into their tenacious clinging to their caste, and so, naturally, into their abhorrence of teaching which tends towards "All ONE in Christ Jesus." It enters into the strength of their family affection, and so into their detestation of a doctrine which makes a man's foes those of his own household.

"Doomed to marry a heathen!"

FROM THE FIGHT.

One must approach them here with the utmost sympathy, and yet we cannot lower the standard and offer them Christ without His Cross. Nor can we dress that Cross in flowers, and hide the thorny Crown.

But the Cross costs so much in India that a new term has been devised to describe those who believe that Christ is the Saviour, and who pray to Him, but who, though of age to choose for themselves, do not come out on His side. Some call them "*Secret Disciples.*"

We, here, do not call them so. We believe discipleship involves open confession,—and disentanglement from the devil's web of caste,—and caste so permeates every action in a Hindu home that no woman can break it without being at once recognised as a Christian, and *this* implies the Cross. Then she has to face the shame. If she lays that Cross down she escapes it—if she takes it up she is forced to go outside the camp bearing His reproach, for no caste woman could ever live as a true Christian at home. It is simply impossible.

We think of these "Secret" ones with tenderness and sympathy, but we cannot call them "disciples." Christ's teaching is far too plain to be mistaken—"Whosoever doth not bear his Cross, and come after Me, cannot be My disciple." And as to the "claim of family ties," the Master

FROM THE FIGHT.

put His claim far first. Ours not to reason why, ours to obey.

Obedience on both sides—ours in faithful teaching, theirs in response, at all costs, means intense suffering. Books could be written about what these Indian women have had to endure, which would thrill the heart of the coldest of English women. God only knows what it means to a Mahommedan or a caste Hindu to be a Christian.

But my work is rather now to tell of the common griefs of every day. Sometimes we fancy that sorrow in itself has a softening influence; we can hardly picture a woman being at the same time sad and bad, but we do not find that sorrow alone does much to move the heart towards God, and often before the message which might draw it near to Him reaches her, the tenderness goes, and defiance comes, and the soul shuts up in the dark of its pain like a lotus flower in the night.

Far away in a great caste town we once saw a widow. She was only a girl of seventeen, with all her life before her, widowed and childless, utterly shamed. She sat alone in an inner room, and brooded over her fate. I shall never forget how she sat, poor child, with her bowed head in her hands. The droop of the white-clad figure told of uttermost weariness. Here,

FROM THE FIGHT.

surely, is one who is ready to come! She will open to Jesu's love! But no, when she looked up and saw us, her face had no welcome in it. It was hard and proud and cold. It was as if the wax had frozen into ice. The only thing that she said to us was, "Would you have me destroy my caste?" It was all that was left to her, poor girl, and to listen to us might mean *that.* Then, with a gesture we could not mistake, she signed to us to go, and she crouched down again, with her head in her hands, and we had to leave her so.

In the same town a woman lived who was longing to be loved. "My husband hates me," she said, "he has taken another wife." But when we spoke of the love of God she laughed, and would not hear. "Tell me anything else you like, but I don't want to listen to *that!*" She was suffering, and in a real way, but Satan had got to her first, and so we had come too late.

There is the suffering of sin. And here one can only "skirt the abyss," one cannot look down into it. The "dark enigma of permitted wrong" is a fearful fact in all heathen lands.

You watch a little child's face change as the flower of her soul withers up. You feel when you go to that house as if Satan were hiding inside, and as if he would thrust out his unclean

FROM THE FIGHT.

hand and clutch you should you go in. But you must go in, for the child is there. Poor little innocent child!

And she comes close to you, and whispers fast, and you feel that horrible hand and shrink back, sick all through at the very thought of what one poor child must bear. For it is sin, sin and sorrow, sorrow and sin, and you go back home again broken down, with all your being strung to the cry, "How long, O Lord! how long!"

But to turn again to the human grief, the simple grief of a stricken soul, who knows no Comforter.

The mother dies, and the children are given over to sorrow. While she was ill they had vowed offerings to the family deities should they come to the rescue and save her, but they were deaf and dumb and far away—"So far away," they say, "that we could not get near them, or move them to answer the prayer that we prayed." Then they wonder how they offended, and in stanza after stanza—for all the Old Indian nature flows out in poetry, and there are different dirges for mother, husband, and child—they plead with the gods to tell them,—to speak but once from their place.

And then comes the Elegy—"*Comparison Song*" they call it, because it is a song of similes. They paint the mother in glowing colours, recounting all she has done for them since they were babes in her arms. And then they bemoan themselves; they are leaves tossed about in rough waters, flowers withered and broken and dead.

But the burden of the dirge for the mother is the thought that they cannot see her, find her, feel her, anywhere. If they had wings they would fly to her; but then, how could they fly for they do not know the way? Where are her footprints to guide them? They search but they find no track!

When she was with them they nestled like little birds under her wing; now, like the jungle birds, they are loosed in some wild, tangled forest, to fight their battles alone.

There is something very desolate about it. The dead form has been borne away to the Burning Ground. They have seen the torch that will light the pyre. They know it is flaming now. To-morrow their mother's ashes will be strewn upon the stream; they will never see her again, they say—for the river flows to the sea.

So they sit for sixteen days—the men and boys may go out and work, but the girls must sit and weep. And this is Sorrow in Heathendom.

" Do you hear them wailing for the dead ? "

We were going to an open-air meeting one evening in the village of the wood, and the sound

FROM THE FIGHT.

of "such as are skilful of lamentation" came from a cottage in the jungle. We stopped and listened.

First came a long, weird wail, like the death cry of spirits departing, then a dirge, the awful, sad, old Tamil dirge for a daughter, then the terrible wail again.

"May I go in?" I asked some men who were sitting silent outside the house. "You may go in," was their answer. "The child of the mother is dead."

Outside it was dusk. Inside it was dark. A few flickering tapers glimmered yellow on bowed heads and swaying forms. The place was full of women, packed so close that there was barely room for me to crouch on the floor among them. They took no notice of me, nor for an instant ceased lamenting. They were all linked the one to the other, and they swung themselves backwards and forwards in perfect rhythmic motion, as they chanted in unison the Dirge for the Dead :—

> "Like a jewel shone her eyes,
> Like red coral were her lips,
> Set with radiant rows of pearl,
>   Yea! her mouth was like a lotus,
>   Like a fair red-water lotus.
>   Whither, whither has she gone?

Then the weird wail rose again and died away like the sound of the winds in the woods.

FROM THE FIGHT.

> "Oh, her hands were living fans,
> Like the graceful wings of swans,
> Girded round with rings of gold.
>> Yea! they helped the poor and needy,
>> Lifted tenderly the fallen.
>> Whither, whither has she gone?

Here the wail broke in, "skilful of lamentation"—God's words describe it best,—and the chant went on—

> "When she wrote, the iron style
> Flashed like lightning in her hand,
> When she spoke, rained golden rain,
>> When she read, like wild bird's music
>> Exquisite the sweet words sounded—
>> Whither, whither has she gone?

Then a pitiful, pitiful bit—

> "Burning sun she could not bear,
> Fall of rain or breath of wind.
> As a flower her mother kept her—
>> Now the fire has scorched and burnt her
>> Driving rain will drench her ashes,
>> Whirlwinds carry them away!

Then with every word a wail—

> "Such a form to fade and fall!
> Such a life to come and go!
> Blown out is the new lit lamp!
>> Half a day could God not spare her?
>> Could not He have waited longer?
>> Nay! He carried her away!"

One's eyes began to see things more clearly as

FROM THE FIGHT.

one grew accustomed to the dim, uncertain light, and one could discern faces and expressions, and see who the real mourners were. The mother sat in the corner, bowed, broken, dumb. She was not wailing. Now she took up the refrain, and the women nearest her beat their breasts and tore their hair as she cried—

" My jewel, my jewel!
My heart's beloved jewel!
Oh, where have you gone?

Then with a paroxysm of wails—

" I search for her—I find her not;
I stretch out my hand in vain!

Then the wailers broke in—

" Oh, never, never more!
You will never see her more!

Then the mother—

" Do you hear me weeping, dear one?
Do you hear me weeping for you?
Does the sound not reach you, touch you,
In the palace of the dead? "

And so the wheel went wearily round. Comfort! They knew it not. This is the Dirge that is sung when a child becomes a Christian. All night long in the jungle outside our house a mother stood and wailed it when her daughter came to us. Only the wail was still bitterer then, and stung by the sting of the shame, she cursed us as she wailed. Had not we stabbed

"The dead form has been borne away to the Burning Ground."

FROM THE FIGHT.

her soul, she cried, when we stole her child away, and woo'd her to love Another One, the Crucified Stranger—Christ!

* * *

A week later, a stone's throw from that jungle hut another woman died.

We had left the village of the wood, but they wrote to us about it,—

"The Heathen watched and wondered, for her husband went singing to the grave!"

To-day he came to see us. "I believe she is with Jesus. He comforted me. *He helped me to let it shine out that He comforted me!*"

"My servants shall sing for joy of heart, but ye shall cry for sorrow of heart." Was ever contrast more vivid? A stroke of God's pen tells it all.

We who have seen it lived out in literal, terrible detail, oh, we long for power to make it live to you! "Oh, God!" we pray as we write it, "do Thou make them see it and feel it! oh, make it so burningly real to them that they will be pressed into prayer! prayer that is fervent, prayer that will cost—for these who are tossed with tempest and not comforted!"

Does prayer make any difference? True prayer does. We have proved God answers prayer. So we plead with you all to pray. "For pity's sake" do we say? No! Pity is not a force

FROM THE FIGHT.

strong enough to inspire and sustain the kind of prayer we need. There is not staying power in it. A stronger force by far is needed to impel a prayer which is to move mountains seven thousand miles away.

Let us look at the woe of the Heathen, the desolate night they live in, whose lives are "walled in with darkness," with eyes which have first seen God's glory, with hearts that can grieve for His sake.

And the Lord says, "Pray . . . Give . . . Go." His Word must be our stimulus.

Do we love Him enough to obey?

Master! Thou seest! Thou knowest!

> "At Thy feet I fall,
> Yield Thee now my all,
> To suffer, live, or die
> For my Lord crucified!"

Phases of Thought

CHAPTER V.

PHASES OF THOUGHT.

> The sound of a sob in the darkness,
> A child crieth after its Father—
> "My spirit within me is burning,
>   Consumed with a passionate yearning—
> Oh, unknown, far away Father!"—
> No voice answers out of the darkness.
>
> THÂYUMÂNAVAR,
> A thousand years ago.
> (Free translation.)

THE people of India think. We talk about "the poor ignorant heathen," and we sing that "the heathen in his blindness bows down to wood and stone," and this is true. There are here, as in every land, the Masses to whom "What shall we eat? and what shall we drink? and wherewithal shall we be clothed?" are matters of infinite moment, and they rarely go beyond them. But there are the Classes. Those who think, and think keenly, who dig deep down into the depths of their marvellous metaphysics—men and women, and children, too, who seem to be born philosophers.

Although it is true that for the most part anything like a ripe knowledge of the Shastras is confined to the men, the more cultured among the women are conversant with them, and almost all of the higher castes are thoroughly imbued with the spirit of Hindu mythology as it is set forth in their ancient literature. Their common talk is full of the Sayings of the Wise, in prose and verse. Their thoughts run on lines quite unfamiliar to Westerns, and the missionary, if she would be equipped for her work, must know something at least of the world of thought expressed in poem and proverb and proverbial allusion, which to the women she wants to win is a very part of themselves. If this is all a closed land to her, she will be so much the further from them, so much the further outside. But this knowledge is not acquired in a year, or in five. One writes humbly, *Not* as though I had already attained!

"Whom do you worship?" we asked a Brahmin widow once. "*Sarvántheriámi*," she answered—*The One who pervades all space, and fills all being.* It is a Sanskrit name for the Eternal God, and is rarely used by the women. It showed in a moment the trend of her thought, and opened the way for a long talk with her upon spiritual things, following along the avenue of ideas already familiar to her.

She held, if I remember right, what is known as the Vedânthic Philosophy, a system of pure Pantheism. To the votaries of this school there is only one great Essence or Entity existent—a sort of vague, misty, impersonal Substance—all else is *Maya*,—delusion.

Their creed is summed up in one phrase, which means " Brahm is all, and all is Brahm." Everything which we see, everything of which our sense takes cognisance, even our own existence and individuality, is a mere mirage, "as though one saw a coil or rope, and fancied it a snake, or seeing nickel silver imagined it pure metal."

Said one who was seeking to discomfit me before his women-folk—" There is only one true Sun, though you may see its virtual image reflected in millions of pools of water. And so those unrealities, which we call souls of men, all illusionary reflections of the one eternal Soul. Is not the atmosphere entire and all pervasive, though men in their puerile folly regard it as divided and confined by material walls and doors? And so the Supreme Soul is one and all pervasive, and it is wisdom's part to regard it as it is, and not as it appears." According to this, in plain language, there is no human Ego. "*I* am not. I do not exist, for the thing that I call 'I' is only an infinitesimal drop in the sea of Infinitude."

"When by austerity and meditation I arrive at this conviction I shall disappear from view, absorbed into the one Original."

This argument leads to the conclusion that since all apparent action is unreal there is no such thing as sin, and therefore Salvation is an empty phrase. No power of argument, nothing but the mighty power of the Holy Ghost can convince a man who holds such a creed, that he is a sinner and needs a Saviour.

The intelligence of the people is shown not only by the subtlety of their system of philosophy, but by the beauty of their poetry, and by their appreciation of it.

Many a rough "Open Air" has been held by an apt word from one of their classics. "As certain also of your own poets have said" has not lost its persuasive power.

I remember one incident well. We were preaching in a large Hindu town, where, as it was market day, some hundreds of people had

FROM THE FIGHT.

gathered round us. They had listened awhile and were restless. We prayed that the Spirit would still them. Then one of our number—a woman—in a clear voice began to sing. Few of them saw who she was, she was hidden by those standing nearest, but they all could hear her song. It ended with an admission of failure to find true rest, for the poet tells how he gathered and scattered the sacred flowers before the idols he thought were gods—all in vain; how he sprinkled libations upon them, but it was all in vain; how he prayed and worshipped in temples —all in vain. Long before she had finished, the crowd was perfectly still, and we had a splendid chance to declare Him unto them.

"Nothing has taken such a lasting hold of the mind of the Tamil people as the terse writings of their Moral Poets. And it is impossible to understand their thought and character without some knowledge of their stanzas." So says a comrade in this South Indian fight.

These stanzas are written in the most nervous and condensed style possible, each word chosen being exactly fitting, and the whole, governed by Eastern laws as to rhyme and rhythm, view it from any point you will, is perfect. Such poems laugh at any attempt to translate them. English sounds very clumsy after Tamil.

But I should like to give you an idea of the

FROM THE FIGHT.

sort of thing that appeals to the Indian mind. "Would you know if the rice is properly cooked? then taste a grain from the cooking pot." The Poetry Pot (to be prosaic) is out of your reach; but a grain or two may suffice to show something of its contents.

One day, some months ago, we got a group of women round us on the verandah of one of their houses. It was not in the caste quarter of the town, and there was no very vigorous resistance till one of them started the common objection that we brought them a *foreign* religion, and after that they were not inclined to listen. One of our number tried to go on in the orthodox way, but they fidgetted under it. Then another took a different tack—"Don't you remember our Avvayar's words?

"'*Twas born with you—that fell disease,*
   'Twill kill you!
From the far foreign mountain the medicine comes,
   'Twill cure you!"

and she repeated the whole verse. They saw the point in a moment, and for fully ten minutes that group of women—all of them poor and illiterate—listened while she told them about the Heavenly Medicine which will cure the disease of sin.

So much for the influence Avvayar wields. She was a poetess, who lived a thousand years

FROM THE FIGHT.

ago. They constantly quote her lines. For example, they are in trouble:

"*Boil it, the milk will lose none of its sweetness;*
Burn it, the shell will grow whiter and whiter;
So will the Good shine brighter and brighter,
The fiercer the fire of their sufferings here."

The other day a Tamil girl was describing a friend who was loyal, as compared with one who was not. This is how the thing struck her:—

"*The water has dried up; where are the water fowl?*
Watch them! Away they soar!
The water has dried up; where are the water plants?
See them! They cling to the shore!
So there are friends who are fickle and faithless,
But some who are true to the core."

Within a few hundred years, more or less (Tamil dates are rather vague), another poet flourished, whose stanzas are household words all over South India to-day. To quote Dr. Pope again: "Tiruvalluvar's poem is one of the select number of great works which have entered into the very soul of a whole people, and which can never die."

We met these lines of his in conversation with a Hindu, who tried to maintain that freedom from all earth-ties, the bond of love included, is the *summum bonum* of true religion.

Read one way they read Truth.

FROM THE FIGHT.

> "*Lay hold on the hold of Him*
> *Who is free from all hold of sin.*
> *I say, lay hold on Him;*
> *So shall the hold of Sin*
> *Lose hold. The hold of Him*
> *Holds from the hold of Sin.*"

The Tamil (which expresses all this in a couple of lines) plays on the word "hold," which really signifies all that holds the soul in the body, all bonds of earthly relationships, all natural ties of affection. We have translated it "hold of sin," because the main idea is that all "hold" is sin.

Think back, if you can, for a thousand years, and see, if you can, that old Tamil poet writing. He is bound by the rules of his art to follow along four lines—Virtue, Wealth, Pleasures, Release—a release which means to him emancipation from births, home, heavenly felicity. He stops when he touches that thought. What does he know of it? *Nothing.* And so he does not write. His book has come down through the ages unfinished, the last long chapter one long blank, the last bar of music—a silence.

Think of him, you to whom the beyond is summed up in one word—CHRIST. *Think of the old Tamil poet thinking alone in the dark.*

We all know Tennyson's picture of the infant crying in the night, and we all know the plaint

FROM THE FIGHT.

of Job: "Oh that I knew where I might find Him, that I might come even to His seat!"

We rarely meet this longing in our work among the Hindus. So far as our experience goes, pictures of "hungry heathen" are absolutely false; but who may say that there never have been such, while this last poem stands. It is infinitely pathetic in the original. There is something in the metre which reminds one of the sound of the moan of the sea.

> " Lord in the darkness I wander,
>   Where is the light ?   Is there no light ?
> Nothing know I, but I wonder,
>   Is there no light ?   Where is the light ?
> Lord, in the vastness I wander,
>   Where is the way ?   Is there no way ?
> How may I reach Thee, I wonder,
>   Is there no way ?   Where is the way ? "

We do not want to make too much of this, because it is not God's call; but is there not something in it to make us stop and think ? "I have but one candle of life to burn, and I would rather burn it *out* where men are dying in darkness than in a land flooded with light."

For a people of such calibre, for all people everywhere, what is wanted? More workers? Yes; but what kind of workers? Will anybody do?

Soul-winning is no child's play even in the

FROM THE FIGHT.

homeland, where we speak our mother tongue, and have to deal with those whose frame of mind we fully understand. In these Eastern lands the battle is the same, but the foe has entrenched himself behind far stronger bulwarks. *The power of Satan is felt to be far more real by all engaged in direct attack.* Our message must be given in a strange and difficult language, and that to a people whose cast of mind is as far removed from ours as the East is from the West. Do not believe the fallacy that anyone will do.

What, then, do the women of Heathendom want?

They want women who will love.

But human love is not enough. It will not stand the strain. Only Divine love lasts. For it is well to face the fact that life out here is just pure plod. There is nothing romantic about it. Only, indeed, it is all lighted up with the light of the joy of our Lord.

They want women who will work.

First comes the language grind. Then the steady doing *and* grind combined. There is nothing exciting in this. A girl who comes out with a vision of picking up the language within her first year, and preaching to interested crowds in her second, is apt to be disappointed.

True Mission Work is not play. It is tremen-

FROM THE FIGHT.

dous earnest. It is not a thing which can be lightly taken up, and laid as lightly down again. "The Vows of God are on me," *and for life.*

But when we think of the needs of China and India, and Africa, all lands of all dark continents, all islands of the sea—oh, we long for a thousand lives for each need, to be "poured forth upon the sacrifice and service!"

Have you thought much of these needs? Have you thought them over one by one in view of the Coming of the King? It is incredible that He wants all these lands to remain as they are in the very depths of the darkness of death, and the question now to be faced is this—*Am I where He means me to be? If not I am missing my life-work. And I may be keeping back blessing from those for whose sake I am staying, by staying with them.*

But we dare not press anyone to come unless she is sure she is called of God, unless she believes in Acts i. verse 8, and unless she means to live only for souls. Once out, the devil's favourite device is to get us engrossed in other things. *Anything* but soul-winning, he says. *Anything* but aggressive fight. And unless the Hand of the Lord is strong upon us we shall give in, and swim with the stream. Compare the thought with "Good *Soldiers* of Jesus Christ."

FROM THE FIGHT.

Comrades who fight from the home side! will you not pray for us? Oh will you not pray the *fervent* prayer that availeth much in its working?

We are not all we would be. As we sketch the woman wanted we feel we fall far short— ' Unto me who am *less than the least of all saints* is this Grace given, that I should preach among the Gentiles the unsearchable riches of Christ."

And so, because He takes the very least, the less than the least, there is nothing to be afraid about. "All God's biddings are enablings." If He calls, fear not, obey.

Here is a verse for the mothers and fathers, and all who give for Jesus' sake. It is also a verse for the sons and the daughters who *ask* them to give for Jesus' sake—It is from Isa. lviii., 10, 11, R.V., margin, "*IF thou bestow on the hungry that which thy soul desireth, THEN the Lord shall satisfy thy soul in dry places.*"

CHURCH OF ENGLAND ZENANA MISSIONARY SOCIETY,
Office: 27, CHANCERY LANE, LONDON, W.C.

ITS ORIGIN.—The Church of England Zenana Missionary Society owes its existence to an earnest desire on the part of Christian Churchwomen to carry out the Saviour's last command by telling their Heathen and Mahommedan sisters of Christ's redeeming love.

This Society is the largest society exclusively employed in working on Evangelical Church lines, wholly for the evangelisation of the women of the East.

Because the women of India, Ceylon and China can be reached by women only, the C. E. Z. M. S. sends forth Women Missionaries only to evangelise their Heathen and Mahommedan sisters in those countries, whose condition, from a Christian standpoint, is lamentable.

ITS WORK.—C. E. Z. M. S. work embraces the following important branches:—

1. **Evangelisation.** Itinerating in hundreds of Hindu, Mahommedan, Singhalese and Chinese villages.
2. **Education.** (1) Women of the secluded classes in their homes. (2) Girls in Schools and Colleges.
3. **Medical Missions, Hospitals and Dispensaries.** Ten of the C. E. Z. M. S. Missionaries are ladies who are fully qualified Medical Practitioners.
4. **Native Agency.** The training of Christian women as Assistant Missionaries, Biblewomen, Dispensers, Nurses and Teachers.
5. **Industrial Missions.** Homes and Classes for Widows and Destitute Women in India and China.
6. **Orphanages.**

ITS NEEDS.—More Prayer, more Subscribers, more Workers at Home and Abroad, more Readers of its Literature, a steady improvement every year in its Income. An Annual Income of **£50,000** is required merely to sustain its present operations, without extension.

Further information on the Society's work, with specimens of the Magazines, will gladly be supplied by the Secretaries,
C.E.Z.M.S., 27, Chancery Lane, London, W.C.

C. E. Z. M. S. Publications.

India's Women and China's Daughters.

The Monthly Illustrated Magazine of the CHURCH OF ENGLAND ZENANA MISSIONARY SOCIETY. Price **One Penny.**
The Magazine to read aloud at Working Parties. Specimen Copies free.
Subscription **1s. 6d.** per annum, post free.

Missionary Gift Books for Adults and Children.

Behind the Pardah.
THE STORY OF C.E.Z.M.S. WORK IN INDIA.
3s. 6d. By IRENE H. BARNES. **2s. 8d.** Nett.
Editor of "India's Women and China's Daughters."

Behind the Great Wall.
By the same Author.
2s. 6d. THE STORY OF C.E.Z.M.S. WORK IN CHINA. **2s.** Nett.

Stories from Mother's Note Book.
By LUCY I. TONGE. Price **2s.** Nett.

A large variety of smaller Books and Booklets, all profusely illustrated, suitable for Bible Class and Sunday School Distribution and Awards.

1s. 6d. **"Not by Might."** **1s. 3d.** Nett.
By the Author of "SEED TIME AND HARVEST."

"Save Some."
C.E.Z.M.S. WORK IN FUH-KIEN. **9d.** Nett.
By MARION HOOK.

6d.
- **Prio's Prayer Answered.**
  By EDITHA F. MULVANY.
- **"He Goeth Before."**
  In Memoriam of a China Missionary, LINDA ROCHFORT WADE.
  By HER SISTER.
- **Gathered Out.**
  THE STORY OF THE BARRACKPORE CONVERTS' HOME.
  By FANNY GOOD.
- **Under Canvas.**
  ITINERATING WORK. By C. HANBURY.

A Cry of Pain.
Medical Mission Booklet. By A. D. Price **1½d.**

THE QUARTERLY ORGAN OF THE SOCIETY.

Daybreak.
Price **1d.** **6d.** per annum, post free.
Specially adapted for young people. Full of Pictures.
Contains Daybreak Workers' Union News.

Please ask for Catalogue of all the New Books, Gratis. Call at Book Room Offices of the Society, 27, Chancery Lane, London, W.C.
Address:—THE LAY SECRETARY, as above.

www.ingramcontent.com/pod-product-compliance
Lightning Source LLC
Chambersburg PA
CBHW020240090426
42735CB00010B/1769